WHERE DO THEY FIT?

Patricia Nell Southern-Musso
Follower Of Jesus Christ

DORRANCE PUBLISHING CO
EST. 1920
PITTSBURGH, PENNSYLVANIA 15238

Dorrance Publishing Co
585 Alpha Drive
Pittsburgh, PA 15238
Visit our website at *www.dorrancebookstore.com*

ISBN: 979-8-8860-4251-1
eISBN: 979-8-8860-4522-2

Contents

Christian Words of Interest

WALK IN THE SPIRIT means that we yield to God's control, we follow His lead, and we allow Him to exert His influence over us. Read. Eph. 4:30 Put to death the deeds of the body by the Spirit. Rom. 8:13.

JUSTIFICATION means God has declared you righteous in His sight.

SANCTIFICATION means God has made you morally right and acceptable.

PRAISE GOD is an expression for our growing reverence for who God is, which, in turn, imparts wisdom to us. We Praise God with our every thought and action.

HALLELUJAH means a way to give God all the honor and glory.

COMMUNION means to commemorate the death of Christ. The bread is for His broken body; and, the juice is for His shed blood. It's also called, "The Lord's Supper."

REDEEMED means being saved or delivered from sin or its consequences.

GLORIFIED means the nature of believers after death and judgement.

GRACE means the spontaneous, unmerited gift of the divine favor in the salvation of sinners, and the divine influence operating in individuals for their regeneration and sanctification.

Lesson One

One of the most important books on Earth: OUR BIBLE.

The Lord has impressed upon my heart to compose this little book to help ANY AND ALL, new or old BELIEVERS in Christ Jesus who know nothing about the Bible or its content.

Some may know the stories of the Bible, but do you know the book itself? Learn that the written Word is Jesus. Your faith is simply believing in the written Word of God and making a daily decision to follow its teaching.

Let's take a few weeks and learn about God's inspired Word. We will learn the books of the Old Covenant and the books of the New Covenant. Also, we will learn a few interesting tidbits along the way. In just six short weeks, you will learn all 66 books of the Bible and other important information that will enhance your spiritual life.

It took a period of 1,500 years through the pen of 40 writers for the Bible to be accomplished. There are 66 books in the entire Bible.

Four hundred years lapsed between the Old Testament and the New Testament. There are a total of 185 songs in the Bible. As of 2019, the Bible has been translated into 698 different languages and just the New Testament in 1,548 languages.

YOU may ask, why the Bible is relevant today?

1. It is a living book (2 Timothy 3:16-17).

2. The wisdom of the Bible is timeless.

3. It's the accuracy of God's Word.

4. The message is clear, compelling, and current.

5. The values and truths of the Bible are timeless.

Wisdom, knowledge, and understanding are found in the Bible. The Bible is important for you because it is God's written revelation of Himself to humanity. The Bible records the history of Israel, Jesus, and the early church. The Bible is a conduit for the Holy Spirit to work in your life today. The bible is not only a book of information, it is a book of transformation.

FIRST, there are two covenants. The Old Testament (O.T.) and the New Testament (N.T.) The O.T. points to the coming of JESUS, and the N.T. tells us about and shows us the works of Christ.

There are 39 books in the Old Testament, and we will learn them in groups of 10:

1.	Genesis	6.	Joshua
2.	Exodus	7.	Judge
3.	Leviticus	8.	Ruth
4.	Numbers	9.	1 Samuel
5.	Deuteronomy	10.	2 Samuel

Repeat:

<table>
<tr><td>1.</td><td>Genesis</td><td>6.</td><td>Joshua</td></tr>
<tr><td>2.</td><td>Exodus</td><td>7.</td><td>Judge</td></tr>
<tr><td>3.</td><td>Leviticus</td><td>8.</td><td>Ruth</td></tr>
<tr><td>4.</td><td>Numbers</td><td>9.</td><td>1 Samuel</td></tr>
<tr><td>5.</td><td>Deuteronomy</td><td>10.</td><td>2 Samuel</td></tr>
</table>

REPEAT out loud several times until you can say them without looking.

WHY is it important to learn the book called THE BIBLE? Because it is the TRUTH concerning your present and eternal life/destination.

The first five books of the Old Testament are called the TORAH, these books are:

1. Genesis
2. Exodus
3. Leviticus
4. Numbers
5. Deuteronomy

These books were written by Moses about 1300 B.C. The TORAH is also known as the PENTATEUCH. The Torah refers to the Law of Moses, or a portion of the law. Sometimes Torah refers to the rules or instructions of a human parent, or of some other wise person (Proverbs 1:8; 3:1).

1. Who wrote the TORAH?

    A. Moses

    B. Joshua

    C. Micah

2. How many years to write the Bible?

    ____

3. How many writers did the Bible have?

    ____

4. How many books in the entire Bible?

    ____

5. The Old Covenant teaches us about?

    ____

    ____

    ____

    ____

6. The New Covenant teaches us about?

    ____

    ____

    ____

    ____

7. TRUE OR FALSE: The first five books of the Old Testament
    are called the Torah.

8. TRUE OR FALSE: The Torah was written by Moses about
    1300 B.C.

REPEAT the first 10 books of the Old Testament?

1. ____________________   6. ____________________

2. ____________________   7. ____________________

3. ____________________   8. ____________________

4. ____________________   9. ____________________

5. ____________________   10. ____________________

On the right side of this page, put these BOOKS in the correct order:

Deuteronomy	1.	____________________
1 Samuel	2.	____________________
Numbers	3.	____________________
Genesis	4.	____________________
Ruth	5.	____________________
Leviticus	6.	____________________
Exodus	7.	____________________
2 Samuel	8.	____________________
Judges	9.	____________________
Joshua	10.	____________________

Congratulations! You have completed your first lesson in learning about God's book called THE BIBLE, our lifeline to eternal life.

The major prophets of the Old Testament are: Isaiah, Jeremiah, Lamentations, Ezekiel, and Daniel. These are described as

"MAJOR" simply because of their length, not because of their significance.

1. Isiah foretold the messiah's coming.
2. Jeremiah pronounced God's judgment upon the people of his time for their wickedness.
3. Lamentations gives us a sacred dignity to the emotions we feel when we see injustice and suffering.
4. Ezekiel means God strengthens. He is often called the father of Judaism. We learn from Ezekiel that the spiritual is just as important as the physical.
5. Daniel is known for remaining loyal to the God of Israel, despite persecution and danger.

The minor prophets are: Hosea, Joel, Amos, Obadiah, Jonah, Micah, Nahum, Habakkak, Zephaniah, Haggai, Zechariah and Malachi. The minor prophets of the Bible are shorter books with more specific content. The role of the prophets was to make God's will known, as well as His HOLINESS, and to instruct God's people to reject IDOLATRY and sin.

YES, LADIES, there were female prophets. Moses' sister, Miriam, is called a "PROPHET" in Exodus 15:20, as are Deborah (Judges 4:4) and Huldah (2 Kings 22:14-20). (REF. Internet, Christianity.com)

God made women for a specific purpose. All things created by God are good, so do not rebel against what God designed.

The story woman embraces her purpose and takes joy and delight in it unapologetically. Women have self-awareness, personal freedom, a measure of self-determination, and personal responsibility for their actions. For Christ, women have an intrinsic (built-in/permanent) value equal to that of men.

Miriam was best known for helping deliver Moses at the Nile River and leading the Hebrew women in singing, dancing, and playing drums after the crossing of the Red Sea. She became critical of Moses's wife because she was a Cushite and God struck her with white leprosy.

Huldah was from the Kingdom of Judah. She was well known for her spiritual perspective. She was called a prophetess.

Deborah was a woman of great wisdom, revelation, and discernment according to the Book of Judges. Deborah was a prophetess of the God of the Israelites, the faith judge of pre-monarchic Israel, and the only female judge mentioned in the Bible.

NOTE: The Bible tells us of 93 women in the Bible who speak. Ninety-four are named. Women are indeed God's most beautiful creation. Women should respect themselves and demand respect from men at all times.

List the major prophets:

1. ____

2. ____

3. ____

4. ____

5. ____

WHAT IS PROPHECY?

A prophecy is a message inspired by God, a divine revelation.
The Bible says that prophets "spoke from God as they
were moved by the Holy Spirit."
2 Peter 1:20-21

So a prophet is one who receives
God's message and transmits it to others.
Acts 3:18

Lesson Two

QUICK REVIEW of last week's lesson:

1. How many writers wrote the Bible?

   ____

2. The Torah consists of how many books?

   ____

3. How many books in the whole Bible?

   ____

4. How many books in the Old Testament?

   ____

5. How many years to complete the Bible?

   ____

6. Name the first 10 books of the Old Testament?

1. ________________	6. ________________
2. ________________	7. ________________
3. ________________	8. ________________
4. ________________	9. ________________
5. ________________	10. ________________

The first printed Bible was by Johannes Gutenberg in the year of 1455 with his associates Johann Fust and Peter Schoeffer. The first printed Bible was in three languages: Hebrew, Aramaic, and Greek; and it took over 1,000 years to complete the Bible, which spanned three continents. These continents were Asia, Africa, and Europe.

Gutenberg first printed 180 Bibles in Mainz, Germany. Forty-nine exist today, and 21 of those are still complete and can be seen at Harry Ransom Center at the University of Texas. Today, the Bible has sold 5 billion copies. It was the first book ever printed, and it was in the Latin language.

GUTENBERG has been called the most influential figure of the last millennium.

NOW we will learn the next 10 books of the Old Testament:

11.	1 Kings	16.	Nehemiah
12.	2 Kings	17.	Esther
13.	1 Chronicles	18.	Job
14.	2 Chronicles	19.	Psalms
15.	Ezra	10.	Proverbs

REPEAT over and over out loud until you are confident they are in your mind.

1. How many languages was the first Bible printed in?

____

2.   Name the languages?

____

3.   Who printed the first Bible?

____

REPEAT the 10 books we are learning today (Books 11-20):

1 Kings	Proverbs
Psalms	Job
Nehemiah	Esther
2 Kings	Ezra
1 Chronicles	2 Chronicles

Now, PUT the books 11-20 in correct order:

11. ___________________   16. ___________________

12. ___________________   17. ___________________

13. ___________________   18. ___________________

14. ___________________   19. ___________________

15. ___________________   20. ___________________

4.   What book comes after Job?

____

5.   What book comes before Nehemiah?

____

6.   What book comes after Esther?

____

REPEAT the 10 books we learned today (Books 11-20). Repetition is the key to learning!

11. _______________________   16. _______________________

12. _______________________   17. _______________________

13. _______________________   18. _______________________

14. _______________________   19. _______________________

15. _______________________   20. _______________________

The Bible is the most stolen book, and it is the bestselling book in the world.

The Bible is the only religious scripture that offers eternal salvation as a free gift, entirely by God's grace and mercy.

In Obadiah 10:15, the term "DAY OF THE LORD" is used by the O.T. prophets to signify a time in the history of mankind when God directly intervenes to bring salvation to His people and punishment to the rebellious. By it, God restores His righteous order in the Earth.

AGAIN REPEAT the 10 books we learned today:

11. _______________________   16. _______________________

12. _______________________   17. _______________________

13. _______________________   18. _______________________

14. _______________________   19. _______________________

15. ___________________   20. ___________________

NOW, REPEAT THE FIRST 20 BOOKS:

1. ___________________   11. ___________________

2. ___________________   12. ___________________

3. ___________________   13. ___________________

4. ___________________   14. ___________________

5. ___________________   15. ___________________

6. ___________________   16. ___________________

7. ___________________   17. ___________________

8. ___________________   18. ___________________

9. ___________________   19. ___________________

10. ___________________   20. ___________________

YES, you can use your Bible.

7. How many books in the whole Bible?

____

8. How many books in the Old Testament?

____

Definition of ATONEMENT in Christianity:

Atonement refers to the needed reconciliation between sinful man and God. This reconciliation is possible through the atoning sacrifice of Jesus Christ, as in Romans 3:25, Romans 5:11, and Romans 5:19. ATONEMENT is the Bible's central message. (REF. Christianity.com)

Psalm 16:10: The sufficiency of Christ's work of atonement is declared in the Resurrection (Romans 6; 2 Timothy 1:10; Hebrews 2:9-18; I Peter 2:18).

By the Resurrection: Jesus was "declared to be the Son of God with power" (Romans 1:4).

He has completed the work He came to do and has ascended to the right hand of the Father. Now we look forward in hope, for having broken the power of death, He has introduced the promise of eternal life to all who receive Him as Messiah (John 6:40; Isaiah 53:1-12).

For New Christians: You now sit together in Christ Jesus in His resurrection. This is not a denominational issue or a point for theological debate. Either we believe Christ rose from the dead and ascended to heaven or we do not. He was able to remove sin and its penalty, if we reject His victory over the grave, we deny ourselves a place in eternity.

You are in Christ in His ascension. Christians believe that after Jesus rose from the dead, He did not die a second time. Instead, 40 days after His resurrection, Jesus left Earth by being taken up, body and soul, to Heaven to rejoin God the Father. This event is called the ascension.

HOLY COMMUNION is a Christian sacrament in which consecrated bread and wine are consumed as the body and blood of Christ as a symbol of a memorial of Christ's death. (REF. Thesaurus)

THE MOST INSPIRING STORY in the Bible is JESUS, the sacrificial lamb. There is no one more inspiring than Jesus. He came to us for a reason, to take our SIN upon Himself in order that we could be blameless in God's eyes. What a divine thrill when a person comes to their senses and realizes that they need a Savior. Even more thrilling is to learn that He is here and has been waiting for you.

ANSWERS TO OBVIOUS QUESTIONS:

How can I be sure that I am saved?

Romans 10:13: Whoever calls on the Lord will be saved.

What if I sin again?

God's provision, 1 John 1:9: He is faithful and just to forgive us. DO NOT go out to sin on purpose; but if we slip ... God is always faithful to forgive.

Will God speak to me?

YES, HE WILL. You hear people say, "Something told me..." Well, that is His still small voice inside warning you.

What is this thing called FAITH?

Faith is deciding that you will trust God to take care of all things in your life. No matter how difficult life becomes, you totally rely on God. FAITH is trusting that God has a good plan and purpose for your life. Faith is taking a risk and stepping out on what you believe God has put in your heart to accomplish. Trust the inner voice within and leap.

GRACE equals God's undeserved approval. (REF. Public Internet)

For He made Him who knew no sin to be sin for us,

that we might become the righteousness of God in Him.

– 2 Corinthians 5:21

Lesson Three

Congratulations! You are absolutely making progress in learning the books of the Bible. You ask, "WHY is this important?" Because you need to know the book you say you believe. Becoming acquainted with God's Word is the most important thing to do with your time. God's Word will be with you when everyone and everything around you has failed.

The King James Bible contains 788,258 words; 31,102 verses; 1,189 chapters; and 66 books.

The diverse background of the writers of the Bible is most interesting. They were farmers, fishermen, tentmakers, homeless prophets, doctors, professional scribes, musicians, and pastors.

Three scientific facts you can find in scripture are:

> Gravity (Job 26:7);
> Water (Job 26:8); and
> Earth's core (Job 28:5).

The Bible has many stories that will absolutely make your eyes bulge out. Take the story of Jonah, now his story is wild, crazy, and true. My favorite story in the Bible.

NOW IT'S TIME TO REVIEW Lessons One and Two

REPEAT the first 20 books of the Bible:

1.	Genesis	11.	1 Kings
2.	Exodus	12.	2 Kings
3.	Leviticus	13.	1 Chronicles
4.	Numbers	14.	2 Chronicles
5.	Deuteronomy	15.	Ezra
6.	Joshua	16.	Nehemiah
7.	Judges	17.	Esther
8.	Ruth	18.	Job
9.	1 Samuel	19.	Psalms
10.	2 Samuel	20.	Proverbs

READ them over in your mind. Now write them here:

1. ______________________   11. ______________________
2. ______________________   12. ______________________
3. ______________________   13. ______________________
4. ______________________   14. ______________________
5. ______________________   15. ______________________
6. ______________________   16. ______________________
7. ______________________   17. ______________________
8. ______________________   18. ______________________
9. ______________________   19. ______________________
10. ______________________   20. ______________________

WRITE them once again. Get them burned into your mind.

1. ___________	11. ___________
2. ___________	12. ___________
3. ___________	13. ___________
4. ___________	14. ___________
5. ___________	15. ___________
6. ___________	16. ___________
7.___________	17. ___________
8. ___________	18. ___________
9. ___________	19. ___________
10. ___________	20. ___________

1. Who wrote the Torah?

   ____

2. How many books in the entire Bible?

   ____

3. How many books in the Old Testament?

   ____

4. Who printed the very first Bible?

   ____

5. TRUE OR FALSE: The Bible was written in three languages.
    If true, NAME them:

1. ___________________________________

2. ___________________________________

3. ___________________________________

Now we learn the next 10 books of the Bible (Books 21-30):

21. Ecclesiastes		26. Ezekiel
22. Song of Solomon		27. Daniel
23. Isaiah		28. Hosea
24. Jeremiah		29. Joel
25. Lamentations		30. Amos

REPEAT. (Write notes to help you remember.)

21. Ecclesiastes		26. Ezekiel
22. Song of Solomon		27. Daniel
23. Isaiah		28. Hosea
24. Jeremiah		29. Joel
25. Lamentations		30. Amos

REPEAT these several times out loud, then write them on these lines:

21. ___________________   26. ___________________

22. ___________________   27. ___________________

23. ___________________   28. ___________________

24. ___________________   29. ___________________

25. ___________________   30. ___________________

God will bless you abundantly for taking time to learn about His BOOK. You are one special person to God, and His favor will shine upon you. God loves you with an everlasting eternal love.

For He made Him who knew no sin to be sin for us,
that we might become the righteousness of God in Him.
– 2 Corinthians 5:21

THE KINGDOM OF GOD, also called Kingdom of Heaven in Christianity, is the spiritual realm over which God reigns, or the fulfillment on Earth of God's will. This occurs frequently in the New Testament, primarily used by Jesus Christ in the first three gospels.

FIVE CHRISTIAN BELIEFS

1. Uniqueness of Christ (Virgin Birth), found in Matthew and Luke.
2. One God, the Trinity (Genesis 1:1, 3:22; Matthew 3:16-17). The Hebrew word for God is "ELOHIM"; this allows for the trinity.
3. Necessity of the Cross (Salvation), found in Matthew 9:6-8; Romans 10:8-10.
4. Resurrection and second coming are together (John 11:25-26; 1 Peter 1:3).
5. Inspiration of Scripture. This is the idea that God "breathed into" biblical writers.

CIRCLE THE BOOKS THAT DO NOT BELONG IN THE OLD COVENANT:

Genesis	Jude	Joel	Mark
Ruth	Luke	Amos	John
Revelation	Acts	Esther	Romans
Numbers	Judges	1 John	Ezra

NOTE: Read the Psalms anytime. The Spirit of the Lord will every time lift you from any worry of life, depression, sadness, illness, etc. As we all know, life can be challenging at times, and we all need that extra touch from a Holy God.

My favorite Psalm is 103.

The book of Psalms has 150 chapters, and as you grow in God's way and continue to read His Word, it will become extraordinary life to your spirit and soul. You also will have a favorite Psalm.

The Spirit of the living God will make you strong and courageous. The Holy Spirit is your partner, your aid, and counselor. He gives you wisdom, understanding, and knowledge. He is your helper in every situation of life. You overcome the devil by the Blood of the Lamb and the word of your testimony. Greater is He (the Spirit of Jesus) that lives in you, than He (the spirit of evil) that is in the world. You are a believer and not a doubter any longer. Feed your faith constantly and starve your doubts to death. Faith comes by hearing and hearing by the Word of God.

Lesson Four

Now that we have successfully completed 30 books of the Old Testament, it is time to finish the process. We will immediately dig into the last nine books of the O.T. after we learn a few interesting tidbits concerning the most important book in the world and renew the first 30 books that we have completed and remembered.

- The great ELIJAH often appeared in the guise of a homeless person.
- Jewish tradition says that ISAIAH suffered martyrdom by being sawn in two under the order of Manasseh.
- JEREMIAH was stoned to death by his exasperated fellow countryman in Egypt.

The men and women in the Bible knew their God, and it should be our goal also. Getting to know His book will begin to bring you closer to Him. God is a Father of mercy and grace, but He also gives out judgment. When we follow God's law, we are blessed. When we disobey, we suffer the curses we find in the book of Deuteronomy. Read about the curses in Deuteronomy, Chapter 28.

REVIEW of the first 30 books of O.T.:

1.	Genesis	16.	Nehemiah
2.	Exodus	17.	Esther
3.	Leviticus	18.	Job
4.	Numbers	19.	Psalms
5.	Deuteronomy	20.	Proverbs
6.	Joshua	21.	Ecclesiastes
7.	Judges	22.	Song of Solomon
8.	Ruth	23.	Isaiah
9.	1 Samuel	24.	Jeremiah
10.	2 Samuel	25.	Lamentations
11.	1 Kings	26.	Ezekiel
12.	2 Kings	27.	Daniel
13.	1 Chronicles	28.	Hosea
14.	2 Chronicles	29.	Joel
15.	Ezra	30.	Amos

A good way to remember is to group them in a way that is easy for you. For example:

Genesis, Exodus, Leviticus, Numbers, Deuteronomy

Joshua, Judges, Ruth, 1 Samuel, 2 Samuel, 1 Kings, 2 Kings

1 Chronicles, 2 Chronicles, Ezra, Nehemiah, Esther

Job, Psalms, Proverbs, Ecclesiastes, Song of Solomon,

Isaiah, Jeremiah, Lamentations, Ezekiel

Daniel, Hosea, Joel, Amos

REPEAT SEVERAL TIMES, and write them here:

1. _________________	16. _________________
2. _________________	17 _________________
3. _________________	18. _________________
4. _________________	19. _________________
5. _________________	20. _________________
6. _________________	21. _________________
7. _________________	22. _________________
8. _________________	23. _________________
9. _________________	24. _________________
10. _________________	25. _________________
11. _________________	26. _________________
12. _________________	27. _________________
13. _________________	28. _________________
14. _________________	29. _________________
15. _________________	30. _________________

Be patient with yourself. You are doing well. Relax and enjoy learning about this most important book. Laugh at yourself, laugh as you mess-up, start all over; it's part of the process. Laughter happens many times in scripture! (Genesis 17:17; Judges 5:11; Psalms 59:8; Job 8:21; 2 Chronicles 30:10; and many other places.)

To complete the Old Testament, we have nine more books to learn (Books 31-39):

31. Obadiah   36. Zephaniah

32. Jonah   37. Haggai

33. Micah   38. Zechariah

34. Nahum   39. Malachi

35. Habakkuk

These will be very easy. Group in three and begin...

Obadiah, Jonah, Micah

Nahum, Habakkuk, Zephaniah

Haggai, Zechariah, Malachi

REPEAT SEVERAL TIMES and then once again.

Now, WRITE THEM ON THESE LINES:

31. _________________   36. _________________

32. _________________   37. _________________

33. _________________   38. _________________

34. _________________   39. _________________

35. _________________

1.   How many men wrote the scriptures?

____

2.   How many years did it take to complete the scriptures?

____

3.   Who wrote the Torah, also called the PENTATEUCH?

   ____

4.   How many books are in the Torah?

   ____

5.   Name the books of the Torah.

   ____

   ____

   ____

   ____

6.   How many books are in the O.T.?

   ____

76. Name the last book in the O.T.

   ____

Congratulations! Pat yourself on the back. You have successfully learned the books of the Old Covenant. God will bless you abundantly above anything you could think or ask. God is good and wants to make your life full of His peace and prosperity.

For He made Him who knew no sin to be sin for us,
that we might become the righteousness of God in Him.
– 2 Corinthians 5:21

Lesson Five

WOW! You have come a very long way. You now know the books of the Old Covenant and now are ready to move ahead with learning about the New Covenant. William Tyndale produced the first printed edition of the New Testament in English.

The New Testament was canonized in the fourth century. The books were written within 50 to 90 years. Jesus fulfilled 300 direct and indirect prophecies of the Old Testament. The New Testament is the fulfillment of the Old Covenant. It relates and interprets the New Covenant, represented in the life and death of Jesus between God and the followers of Christ, the promised Messiah.

The five major milestones in the New Testament narrative of the Life of Jesus are His Baptism, transfiguration, crucifixion, resurrection, and ascension.

1. BAPTISM (Matthew 3:13-17).

2. TRANSFIGURATION (Matthew 17:1-3). While the verb transfigured may denote spiritual transformation in Romans 12:2, here it indicates a visible transformation, affirming the essential glory of Jesus the Messiah.

3. CRUCIFIXION (Matthew 27:15-22).

4. RESURRECTION (Matthew 28:1-15; John 20:1-18).

5. ASCENSION (Ephesians 8:7-10; Acts 1:9-11).

There are 93 women who speak in the Bible, 49 are named. They speak a total of 14,056 words. There are a total of 188 named women in the Bible. Jesus first told a woman to, "Go and tell" everyone that HE HAS RISEN.

HERE WE GO! Put on your memory hat. There are 27 books in the New Testament. This week, we will learn 14 books. These are easy to remember. So relax.

1.	Matthew	8.	2 Corinthians
2.	Mark	9.	Galatians
3.	Luke	10.	Ephesians
4.	John	11.	Philippians
5.	Acts	12.	Colossians
6.	Romans	13.	1 Thessalonian
7.	1 Corinthians	14.	2 Thessalonians

GROUP these as:

Matthew, Mark, Luke, John, Acts, Romans

1 Corinthians, 2 Corinthians, Galatians, Ephesians

Philippians, Colossians, 1 Thessalonians, 2 Thessalonians

REPEAT out loud several times, then do this simple quiz below. YES, you can look.

1.   What is the third book in the New Testament?

____

2.   TRUE or FALSE: There are two Colossians.

____

3.   Name the first book in the New Testament.

____

GO BACK to repetition. Repeat over and over again until you have them in your mind:

   Matthew, Mark Luke, John, Acts, Romans

   1 Corinthians, 2 Corinthians, Galatians, Ephesians

   Philippians, Colossians, 1 Thessalonians, 2 Thessalonians

CIRCLE THE BOOKS THAT DO NOT BELONG IN THE NEW COVENANT:

Mark	Amos	John	Jonah
Jude	Luke	Numbers	Romans
Esther	Genesis	Matthew	Ruth

The gospels, which are Matthew, Mark, Luke, John, tell the life of Jesus and His teachings.

The Book of Acts details the work of Jesus' followers in propagating the Christian Faith while the Epistles teach about the meaning and implications of Faith.

The Book of Revelation gives prophecies about future events and the culmination of divine purpose.

On the right, PUT the books in correct ORDER (YES, you can look if needed!):

Ephesians	1. _______________
1 Thessalonians	2. _______________
Philippians	3. _______________
2 Thessalonians	4. _______________
Colossians	5. _______________
Galatians	6. _______________
Matthew	7. _______________
Acts	8. _______________
Mark	9. _______________
Romans	10. _______________
Luke	11. _______________
John	12. _______________
1 Corinthians	13. _______________
2 Corinthians	14. _______________

The New Testament refers to a New Covenant that Christians believe completes or fulfills the MOSAIC Covenant (the Old Covenant) that YAHWEH (the National God of Israel) made with the people of Israel on Mount Sinai through Moses.

Remember: Who was Moses? He wrote the Torah, the first five books of the Old Covenant.

You are doing great. Now let us continue on to the finish, learning just WHERE DO THEY FIT?

All the books of the Bible—in the Old Covenant OR the New Covenant?

Lesson Six

We are on our last leg of learning all 66 books of the Bible. The last 13 books will be as easy as all the rest. Only now, you have a knowledge/routine of just how to group books together in order to learn quickly. There are some great stories in the New Testament:

- Peter walking on the water, found in Matthew 14:25-28. Now that took a lot of courage and faith!

- John 3:16: For God so loved the world. This is hard for humankind to totally comprehend. It is a true statement that we all have to believe OR else we probably will not be saved. God's love for us is absolutely amazing. He loved us while we were in sin.

- The Transfiguration, found in Matthew 17:1-4. What an incredible event to observe! Jesus defying gravity and rising straight upward. Yes, I would have loved to be there.

REVIEW of first 14 books of New Covenant. Let's GO!

1.	Matthew	8.	2 Corinthians
2.	Mark	9.	Galatians
3.	Luke	10.	Ephesians
4.	John	11.	Philippians
5.	Acts	12.	Colossians

6. Romans

7. 1 Corinthians

13. 1 Thessalonians

14. 2 Thessalonians

Repetition and more repetition!

GROUPS:

Matthew, Mark Luke, John, Acts, Romans

1 Corinthians, 2 Corinthians, Galatians, Ephesians

Philippians, Colossians, 1 Thessalonians, 2 Thessalonians

WRITE THEM HERE:

1. _______________________

2. _______________________

3. _______________________

4. _______________________

5. _______________________

6. _______________________

7. _______________________

8. _______________________

9. _______________________

10. _______________________

11. _______________________

12. _______________________

13. _______________________

14. _______________________

REPEAT ONCE AGAIN.

Traditionally, 13 of the 27 books in the New Testament were attributed to Paul, the apostle who famously converted to Christianity after meeting Jesus on the road to DAMASCUS and wrote a series of letters that helped spread the faith throughout the Mediterranean world.

The New Testament is the second division of the Christian biblical canon. It discusses the teachings and person of Jesus, as well as events in first-century Christianity.

Now it is time to complete our study of the biblical books and WHERE DO THEY FIT?

The remaining 13 books are:

15. 1 Timothy	22. 2 Peter
16. 2 Timothy	23. 1 John
17. Titus	24. 2 John
18. Philemon	25. 3 John
19. Hebrews	26. Jude
20. James	27. Revelation
21. 1 Peter	

This group will be easy to remember, because they group easily. Try remembering them like this:

1 Timothy, 2 Timothy, Titus

Philemon, Hebrews, James

1 Peter, 2 Peter

1 John, 2 John, 3 John

Jude, Revelation

As we have learned during these lessons: repetition and grouping; and more repetition!

REPEAT the above books several times, then write them here from memory if possible.

15. ____________________   22. ____________________

16. ____________________   23. ____________________

17. ____________________   24. ____________________

18. ____________________   25. ____________________

19. ____________________   26. ____________________

20. ____________________   27. ____________________

21. ____________________

On the right, put books 15 through 27 in the correct order:

Revelation	15. ____________________
James	16. ____________________
3 John	17. ____________________
Philemon	18. ____________________
Titus	19. ____________________
Hebrews	20. ____________________
1 John	21. ____________________
1 Peter	22. ____________________
2 John	23. ____________________
Jude	24. ____________________
1 Timothy	25. ____________________
2 Timothy	26. ____________________
2 Peter	27. ____________________

FIVE teachings of Jesus will improve your life:

1. LOVE God and your neighbor.

2. LIVE the Golden Rule, found in Matthew's gospel: treat other as you want to be treated.

3. Have FAITH in Jesus Christ.

4. Communicate with God.

5. Freely FORGIVE.

BRIEF TEST

Put N.T. or O.T. beside these books.

EXAMPLE: Revelation=N.T.

Hebrews	_______	Genesis	_______
Numbers	_______	Titus	_______
James	_______	Job	_______
Proverbs	_______	Ezra	_______
Esther	_______	Luke	_______
Acts	_______	Hosea	_______
Philemon	_______	Romans	_______
Ezekiel	_______	Song of Solomon	_______

For He made Him who knew no sin to be sin for us,

that we might become the righteousness of God in Him.

– 2 Corinthians 5:21

God's righteousness that is, right standing with Him,

comes through FAITH in Christ alone.

– Romans 10:3

ALL references for this lesson guide found in: *Spirit Filled Life Bible.*

THE APOSTLES' CREED:
is one of the first of these statements
and it identifies and states the most essential of
Christian doctrine. The Apostles' Creed professes
what Christians believe about the persons and
work of God the Father, God the Son,
and God the Holy Spirit.

Six Days of Creation

Genesis 1:2:

The earth was without form and void; darkness was on the face of the deep; and the Spirit of God was hovering over the face of the waters. Then God said, "LET THERE BE LIGHT," and there was light. God divided the light from the darkness. This was the FIRST DAY.

Genesis 1:6:

Then God said, "LET THERE BE A FIRMAMENT IN THE MIDST OF THE WATERS, and let it divide the waters from the waters." This was the SECOND DAY.

Genesis 1:9-13:

Then God said, "Let the waters under the heavens be gathered together into one place, and let the dry land appear," and it was so. God called the dry land Earth, and the gathering together of the waters He called seas. And God saw that it was good. Then God said, "Let the earth bring forth grass, the herb that yields seeds, and the fruit tree that yields fruit according to its kind, whose seed is in itself, on the earth." And the earth brought forth grass, the herb that yields seed according to its kind, and the tree that yields fruit, whose seed is in itself according to its kind. And God saw that it was good. So the evening and the morning were the THIRD DAY.

Genesis 1:14-19:

Then God said, "Let there be lights in the firmament of the heavens to divide the day from the night; and let them be for signs and seasons, and for days and years; and let them be for lights in the firmament of the heavens to give light on the earth," and it was so. Then God made two great lights; the greater light to rule the day and the lesser light to rule the night. He made the stars also. God set them in the firmament of the heavens to give light on the earth, and to rule over the day and over the night, and to divide the light from the darkness. And God saw that it was good. So the evening and the morning were the FOURTH DAY.

Genesis 1:20-23:

Then God said, "Let the waters abound with an abundance of living creatures, and let birds fly above the earth across the face of the firmament of the heavens." So God created great sea creatures and every living thing that moves, with which the waters abounded according to their kin, and every winged bird according to its kind. And God saw that it was good. And God blessed them, saying, "Be fruitful and multiply, and fill the waters in the seas, and let birds multiply on the earth." So the evening and the morning were the FIFTH DAY.

Genesis 1:24-31:

Then God said, "Let the earth bring forth the living creature according to its kind; cattle and creeping things and beast of the earth, each according to its kind," and it was so. And God made the beast of the earth according to its kind, cattle according to its kind, and everything that creeps on the earth according to its kind. And God saw that it was good.

Then God said, "Let us make man in OUR IMAGE according to Our likeness; let them have dominion over the fish of the sea, over the birds of the air, and over the cattle, over all the earth and over every creeping thing that creeps on the earth." So God created man in His own image; in the image of God He created him; male and female, He created them. Then God blessed them, and God said to them, "Be fruitful and multiply; fill the earth and subdue it; have dominion over the fish of the sea, over the birds of the air, and every living thing that moves on the earth." And God said, "See, I have given you every herb that yields seed that is on the face of all the earth, and every tree whose fruit yields seed; to you, it shall be for food. Also, to every beast of the earth to every bird of the air, and to everything that creeps on the earth, in which there is life, I have given every green herb for food"; and it was so. Then God saw everything that He had made, and indeed it was very good. So the evening and the morning were the SIXTH DAY.

NOTE: Ultimately, God has given each of us free will to choose what we believe. But He has placed His fingerprints all over His creation, and He has written an instruction manual, so we will know how to live (Psalm 19:1, 119:11; 1 Peter 2:11-12). His Word has given us ample evidence that it can be trusted, and those who trust the Bible have a solid foundation upon which to build their lives (Matthew 7:24-28).

Psalm 103:1-3 Bless the Lord, O my soul; and all that is within me, bless His holy name! Bless the Lord, O my soul, and forget not His benefits. God forgives all your iniquities and heals all your diseases.

Most Important Decision

Some years ago, it was a fad for young teens to greet one another with the word "YOLO." Now, this may be a cute, unique greeting, but it has no basis for truth. It means "you only live once," so go out and party hard, wildly live your life, etc. Well! The fact is that we all live forever, either in heaven or hell. We make that decision while we journey on this Earth. The way to accept Jesus as your personal Savior is to follow the simple guide below. To be saved, you must turn away from sin, believe in the death and resurrection of Jesus, and receive Him as Lord and Savior of your life.

FIRST, you must consider your life and then turn away from everything in it that is contrary to what God wants. This turning away from selfishness and toward God is called REPENTANCE (Matthew 3:7-10; Acts 3:19).

SECOND, you must acknowledge that Jesus Christ died on the Cross to forgive you of sin. You take Him as your Savior to cleanse you from sin—as the substitute who paid the price due for your sin (Romans 5:9-10; Titus 2:14)

THIRD, you must ask Him to be Lord of your life, acknowledging openly and verbally that Jesus is not only your Savior but your Lord (1 John 2:23). (REF. *Spirit Filled Life Bible*)

NOTE: Abundantly forgiven by God, we are to abundantly forgive.

1.   In our receiving God's love and merciful forgiveness.

2.   In our giving it, just as we have received.

Two virtues, goodness and forgiveness, are attributes birthed by our Heavenly Father and expected to be in our own lives.

God does not want us to portion out our mercy and forgiveness with teaspoons. He wants people to show forth their faith, mercy, and forgiveness with dump truck loads.

Pray This Prayer

Father, in Jesus' name, I come to You as a sinner asking for Your forgiveness. I am sorry for my sin and total rebellion against Your way and want to repent now. Come into my heart and be Lord over my life. Your Word teaches that if anyone will ask for Your mercy and grace, that You will not turn them away. Thank you for coming into my heart and saving me from eternal damnation. Amen.

What is Hell Like?

Luke 16:23:

There are two descriptions of hell in the Bible. One is of a burning fire. Jesus often used the word GEHENNA to describe hell. Gehenna was a refuse dump outside Jerusalem that was always on fire. Jesus said hell was a place of worms, maggots, fire, and trouble. Jesus also said that hell would be "outer darkness...weeping and gnashing of teeth" (Matthew 8:12). It is a place of terrible loneliness, separation from God and man. Believe me, you do not want to take a chance on missing Heaven. (REF. SFLB)

What Is Truth?

It is something upon which a person may confidently stake his life. The truth of God's Word is certain, stable, rightness and trustworthiness.

TIMELY NOTE: At this specific time in the history of the world, the coming of the Lord could be any moment. Biblical prophecy is falling into place very quickly. This is March 5, 2022, and at this very moment, there is WAR going on between Russia and Ukraine. Russia has invaded the Ukraine and trying to overtake their country, The threat of nuclear war is in the air. Every nation on planet Earth is feeling the extreme discomfort/ruthlessness/ pure evil of this Russian dictator. This could be the beginning of

WWIII. Only God knows the end from the beginning concerning this invasion of Ukraine. Absolutely, today is your day for salvation.

TODAY, March 11, 2022, it is snowing rapidly in the boonies of Oklahoma. It is beautiful, white, and pure. The Lord impressed upon me that when He cleanses the very vilest of sinners, that is how His blood cleanses them. They become clean and pure as the whitest snow. God loves and will accept you IF you will just repent of your sin and make a complete 180-degree turn. God is NOT MAD at anyone; He desires that all people everywhere repent and run into His loving arms. The Russian and Ukraine war is still ongoing; may the Lord God intervene supernaturally and stop this insanity. The whole world is just watching while Putin, the dictator of Russia, destroys the Ukraine and murders its people. God in Heaven help us all.

John 6:28-29:

The people placed primary emphasis on their works for God and on God's works for them (signs), whereas Jesus' singular focus is on believing (that is, trusting) in the One whom God sent.

The people said to Him: "What shall we do, that we may work the works of God?"

Jesus said: "This is the work of God, that you believe in Him whom He sent."

Very simple, just believe.

Twenty Tips for New Christians to Grow in Faith

1. Get connected to a community of believers.

2. Get baptized.

3. Start a regular prayer life.

4. Share your faith with everyone.

5. Read the Word and find God's promise for you.

6. Meditate on God's Word.

7. Journal your favorite verses.

8. DO NOT expect to have all the answers or become perfect.

9. On a regular basis, confess your sin to God.

10. Bask in the freedom that comes with the grace of God and let go of guilt of past transgressions.

11. Reflect on your life and see if you need to change your lifestyle to honor God.

12. Mend relationships.

13. DO NOT expect overnight change.

14. Surround yourself with scripture verses.

15. DO NOT be afraid to ask questions.

16. Find a mentor. They hold you accountable and help you to grow in Christ.

17. Find a Bible believing church and get involved.

18. Start your day by giving THANKS to God.

19. Having a spiritual mentor is very important. Be open and honest with each other.

20. Keep seeking the Lord.

GOD LOVES YOU!

You did not choose Me, but I chose you
and appointed you that you should go and bear fruit,
and that your fruit remains, that whatever you ask
the Father in My name He may give you.
– John 15:16

REMEMBER NEW/ALL BELIEVERS: When we abide in Christ, our prayers are effective; we glorify God in our fruit bearing; we demonstrate our discipleship; and our joy becomes full through experiencing Christ's own joy within us (John 15:7-11).

Ten Things
Every New Believer Should Know

1. God loves us. The one thing that the Bible emphasizes more than us loving God and people is that God loves us. He loves us first and most.

2. Relationships first. Your motivation and the purpose of learning, serving, worshipping, giving, teaching, reading, praying, etc. to grow relationally more is to love with God and people (Matthew 22:36-40).

3. You not only are saved by GRACE, you grow by it, too. A common trap for new and older Christians is trying to clean up their lives without God's help. The less you sin, the less you need God's grace. You can't sin less and love more without the strength of God's grace.

4. DO NOT trample over the great commandment trying to obey the Great Commission. Instead, lead people to JESUS by loving people to Him (1 Corinthians 13:1-3).

5. Love your neighbor. Your literal neighbors. Do this because you are a Christian, not just because you want them to be Christians.

6. It is all about JESUS. Jesus is God who became a man. He is the center and circumference, the hub and rim of life and creation. FOCUS on Jesus, His cross, His resurrection, and His Kingdom.

7. God cares about your whole life. God cares about and is Lord of all your life: personal, emotional, social, family, financial, physical, vocational, sexual, and intelligent.

8. Love other Christians even when they are different.

9. Pray with the Bible open. Spiritual exercises are fasting, solitude, serving. The two most important things are communicating and communion with God through praying and listening to and learning about God through the Holy Scriptures.

10. Find a Christian mentor. ASK an older Christian to mentor you. They are always glad to help new believers.

(REF. Public Internet)

Psalm 19:7:

The complete trustworthiness of the Bible. The Word of God. That "the law of the Lord is perfect" is direct reference to the absolute, complete, and entire trustworthiness of the Holy Scriptures, which constitute the Bible. The Word of God is perfect in its accuracy and sure in its dependability. Two terms are generally used to describe these features of God's Word:

1. INERRANT PERFECT means that, in the original copies of each manuscript written by each Bible book's respective author, there was nothing mistaken or tinged with error. Further, the excellence of the Holy Spirit's protection of the scriptures over the centuries has ensured that the copies delivered into our hands from generations past are essentially the same. Even literary critics who claim no faith in the truth of the Bible attest to its

being the most completely reliable of any book trans-
mitted from antiquity in terms of it actually remaining
unchanged and dependably accurate.

2. INFALLIBLE refers to the fact that the Bible is unfailing
as an absolutely trustworthy guide for our faith (belief
in God) and practice (life and behavior). This is so because God is true (John 3:33; 17:3) and because God
cannot lie (Numbers 23:19; Titus 1:2; Heb. 6:18).

(REF. SFLB, p. 768)

STAY on the narrow path of following the Lord Jesus Christ. Your
life will be much better now, plus you will reap eternal benefits. God
is always good, and He has a good plan and purpose for your life.

Back in 1983 when I received Jesus into my heart, it was so
exciting, thrilling, and absolutely amazing that it became my in-
tention to tell the whole world. Little did I know that the world
did not really want to learn about the most incredible TRUTH
in the universe. They are blinded to the truth that can set them
free from the bondage of sin. Any type of sin (no matter what it
may be) is cooperating with Satan in his nature and manifesting
his works in/on the Earth. IF you stay in sin long enough, you
will begin to see into that ugly, demonic realm of darkness.

Anyway, my prayer at that time was for a mentor to teach me
God's way, and that prayer was answered. The first three to five
years of my spiritual journey, God placed various mentors in my
life to help me learn, pray, worship, and stand on the Word of
God. It was a glorious time. Those dear ladies will always be so
special in my heart. Anxious to meet them one day in Heaven

and let them know that their work in my personal life was not in vain, it is my belief that God will show me His abundant goodness/blessings in the land of the living.

NOW that you are a new believer in Christ Jesus, YOU sit together in Christ Jesus in His Resurrection. Now, resurrection is not a denominational issue or a point for theological debate. Either we believe Christ rose from the dead and ascended to Heaven or we do not. Jesus' resurrection proved He was able to remove sin and its penalty. If we reject His victory over the grave, we deny ourselves a place in eternity.

ASCENSION:

In His ascension, Christians believe that after Jesus rose from the dead, he did not die a second time. Instead, 40 days after His resurrection, Jesus left the Earth by being taken up body and soul to heaven to rejoin God the Father. This event is called the Ascension.

His present rule at God's right hand means He has conquered death. He is in the highest place of honor and shares in God's strength, authority, and blessing. It means He is now Priest and King. He will one day return to Earth to rule, just as the Holy Scripture teaches.

A Brief Bio of My Life

My birth happened in December 1940. I grew up and went to school in a very small farming community in Oklahoma. My life was full of fun and friends, playing ball, playing with my dolls, hide and seek; plus other outside games. It was a life of amazement, adventure and summer thrill; until, that horrific Sunday afternoon when my childhood became a total nightmare from the pits of hell. The innocence of my childhood was over, never to be regained. Like most little girls growing up, life was puzzling. The people who were supposed to protect/love me were the ones hurting me. I was sexually abused by an older relative for many years. It was not only me, but other little girls in the community. He kept us quiet by putting such fear into our hearts. He told us if we told anyone what he did to us, our parents would not love us anymore and would probably send us away because we were bad girls. He constantly fed into us that it was our fault for his being a child-molester, that we made him do such things to our little bodies. He was an evil and perverted man, but he knew how to hide his evil by being one of the outstanding members in the local church. Immediately after church he would find one of the little girls in the community and begin his perversion. His perversion continued until my parents moved out of the community to another state.

My teen life was like any other, going to school, dating, part-time work, and helping with family. My dating years were full of turmoil because I did not trust males. It was not easy, and I credit my mother's prayers for finding the right husband. Both of my parents worked at night, and it was my responsibility to care for a young sister. Later in my life, it was my opportunity to have one-and-a-half years of Bible college and also various college computer classes.

After high school, I went to a Vo-Tech to learn keypunch/computer operations. This was a new enterprise coming into society back in the late fifties and sixties. People were afraid of them because no one knew anything about or had heard much about computer technology. Upon completion of these classes, it was time to find a job. Now that was a task. Finally, I landed my first job at Standard Insurance Company, and that is where I met my husband. Like most marriages, we had many ups and downs, but always decided to work through the problems and make it work, which is exactly what we did. We were married for 59 years. We have one beautiful daughter and one grandson, whom we both love dearly.

I helped care for elderly parents and my husband until their deaths. Now, being a widow, my days are filled with church, travel, volunteering, friends, and composing this little book.

My spiritual birth came in December 1983. Without God in your life, it becomes unbearable. Because of sin, my life had become shambles. These words to an old song fit me best. The song goes like this: "I was sinking deep in sin, far from a peaceful shore, very deeply stained within, sinking to rise no more; but the Master of the sea heard my despairing cry, from the waters lifted me, now safe am I, love lifted me."

Yes, His love lifted me, and can lift you, out of any pit you may find yourself in. IF you are bound by lust, alcohol, drugs, sale of women and children, envy, gossiping, womanizing, or whatever you find yourself trapped within—the lust of the flesh, the lust of the eyes, or the pride of life—remember it is Satan who is trying to kill you. The Gospel of Jesus will set you free.

My whole life changed when Jesus came into my heart. All colors became brighter, the desires of my heart changed, the way I looked at people changed, and the craving to learn the Bible was foremost in my mind. Jesus lifted me from the pits of hell. YES, I fell into dark, sick, immoral sin, just like most of you reading my book, but I am a living witness to the forgiveness, mercy, love, and grace of our Lord Jesus Christ. He will pick you up and give a reason to continue living. The Lord has used me in children's ministry, nursing home ministry, home cell groups, prayer ministry, and local and foreign missions work. He also has a place just for you. Run forward in your new life and look for open doors to serve. Believers in Christ Jesus will commit great sin once in a while, but when this happens in your life, just remember 1 John 1:9: this is the cleansing scripture for fallen believers. IF we confess our sins, He is faithful and just to forgive us our sins and to cleanse us from all unrighteousness. IF we say that we have not sinned, we make Him a liar, and His word is not in us. A true believer WILL NOT continue in habitual sin.

The details of my sin and the depth to which my soul sank are not important, but what is important is that Jesus saved me just in time. He is now calling your name. Receive Him into your heart and soul this day.

NOTE: By the time my little book hits the bookstore shelves, I will have turned 82 years of age. This is my dream to leave a book for humanity to read in order to tell them about Jesus and what He did in my personal life. My hair is snow white; blue eyes; five-feet, two-inches tall.

During my Christian walk, God has been extremely good to me. He provided mentors during my early years of following Christ. One of my mentors told me, "IF you want your prayers answered, KEEP YOUR TONGUE FROM EVIL," which is gossip. An ungodly man digs up evil. Death and life are in the power of the tongue (Proverbs 18:21). To live a victorious life, wait and trust upon the Lord. It has been my opportunity to have books, tapes, and television ever so available. The Lord has helped me to hear what the BIG TIME ministers on TV are teaching and how to apply it to my life. God is good. Use whatever is in your hands for the GLORY OF GOD. My belief is that God will show me His abundant blessings in the land of the living.

The Ten Commandments

YES, you need to know them because they help you to know that you need a Savior for you life. Humanity has committed this list of sins. The Bible declares that if you have only committed one, then you have committed all. LEARN these and teach your children.

EXODUS 20:1-17 (*Spirit Filled Life Bible*):

1. You shall have no other gods before ME.
2. You shall not make for yourself a carved image.
3. You shall not take the name of the Lord your God in vain.
4. Remember the Sabbath day, to keep it holy.
5. Honor your father and your mother (only one with a promise).
6. You shall not murder (Matthew 5:22: This extends to thought and word, to unrighteous anger and destructive insults).
7. You shall not commit adultery (Matthew 5:27-28: Lusting in your mind and heart is committing the act). Any sexual activity outside of marriage between a man/woman is adultery. Adultery is absolutely spiritual rebellion against a Holy God. Adultery is for sure having intercourse with Satan himself. Man and woman living

together outside of marriage is called fornication. ("Shacking-up," also forbidden by God.) There are many sins against a Holy God beside adultery.

8. You shall not steal.

9. You shall not bear false witness against your neighbor (instead, always be trustworthy and truthful).

10. You shall not covet your neighbor's house, wife, or male/female servant or anything else.

And this is His commandment, that we should believe
on the name of His Son Jesus Christ and love one another,
as He gave us commandment.
Now he who keeps His commandments abides in Him,
and He in him. And by this we know that He abides in us,
by the Spirit whom He has given us.
– 1 John 3:23-24, SFLB

NOTE: When we are assured of our standing before God, it gives us boldness in prayer. When we keep His commandments, we give evidence that we are in harmony with God's will. The indwelling Holy Spirit manifests His presence outwardly in our life and conduct, giving evidence of our relationship with God. (REF. SFLB, p. 1931)

CHRISTIANS believe that because of the omnibenevolent nature of God, He gives human beings instructions on how to live a good life and get to heaven after they die. According to Christian belief, the Ten Commandments are important RULES from God that tell Christians how to live in obedience to God, worship to Him, and get closer to Him.

And why do you look at the speck in your brother's eye,
but not consider the plank in your own eye?
– Matthew 7:3

Judge not, that you be not judged.

Matt. 7:1

The Nine Beatitudes

"BLESSED" comes from the root "MAKARIOS," indicating large or of long duration. The word is an adjective suggesting happiness; supremely blessed is a condition in which congratulations are in order. It is a grace word that expresses the special joys and satisfaction granted the person who experiences salvation.

MATTHEW 5:1-12:

- Blessed are the poor in spirit, for theirs is the kingdom of heaven.
- Blessed are those who mourn, for they shall be comforted.
- Blessed are the meek, for they shall inherit the earth.
- Blessed are those who hunger and thirst for righteousness, for they shall be filled.
- Blessed are the merciful, for they shall obtain mercy.
- Blessed are the pure in heart, for they shall see God.
- Blessed are the peacemakers, for they shall be called sons of God.
- Blessed are those who are persecuted for righteousness' sake, for theirs is the kingdom of heaven.
- Blessed are you when they revile and persecute you and say all kinds of evil against you falsely for My sake.

- Rejoice and be exceedingly glad, for great is your reward in Heaven, for so they persecuted the prophets who were before you.

THE POOR IN SPIRIT are those who recognize their spiritual poverty and, casting aside all self-dependence, seek God's grace.

MOURNING are not necessarily people in bereavement, but those who experience the sorrow of repentance.

MEEK does not connote weakness, but rather controlled strength. The word carries the ideas of humility and self-discipline.

God is the supreme Peacemaker, and His sons follow His example.

The cause of persecution is loyalty to righteousness, which Jesus makes specific in 5:11.

IMPORTANT NOTE: The Beatitudes help us today as we remember to embrace the importance of living the TRUTHS each day. In short, the Beatitudes tell us that the good action we do will be rewarded in the afterlife, and through our lifetime.

(REF. Notes found in the *Spirit Filled Life Bible*, p. 1410)

The Twelve Apostles

"DISCIPLE" is from the verb "MANTHANO," "to learn," whose root—"math"—suggests thought with effort put forth. A disciple is a learner, one who follows both the teaching and the teacher. The word is used first of the 12 disciples and later of Christians generally. (Revelation; Matthew 10, SFLB, p. 1421)

First Simon, who is called Peter, and Andrew his brother; James the son of Zebedee and John his brother; Philip and Bartholomew; Thomas and Matthew the tax collector; James the son of Alphaeus, and Lebbaeus, whose surname was Thaddaeus; Simon the Cananite and Judas Iscariot, who also betrayed Him. (Matthew 10:1-4, SFLB)

Peter	Andrew	James
John	Philip	Bartholomew
Thomas	Matthew	James
Thaddaeus	Simon	Judas

Matthew summarizes the Galilean ministry of Jesus and introduces the commission He gave to His disciples. Jesus bestows upon His 12 disciples the delegated POWER that He Himself possessed, that is "authority" to advance the messianic ministry through exorcism healing.

REPEAT them several times to yourself, then write them here:

1. ______________	7. ______________
2. ______________	8. ______________
3. ______________	9. ______________
4. ______________	10. ______________
5. ______________	11. ______________
6. ______________	12. ______________

NOW close your eyes and see them in your mind:

Peter	Andrew	James
John	Philip	Bartholomew
Thomas	Matthew	James
Thaddaeus	Simon	Judas

MAIN TEACHING FROM THE APOSTLES:

To teach the message of faith, repentance, and baptism; to bear witness to the divine mission of the SAVIOR; to outline man's relationship to Jesus and to God our Father; to strengthen testimonies and divine doctrine; and to reinforce the teachings of the Christian church.

The Seven Churches of the Apocalypse

THE SEVEN CHURCHES OF THE APOCALYPSE

1. EPHESUS (Revelation 2:1-7)

   Commendation: Rejects evil perseveres, has patience.

   Criticism: Their love for Christ was no longer fervent.

   Instruction: Do the works you did at first.

   Promise: They would receive the tree of life.

2. SMYRNA (Revelation 2:8-11)

   Commendation: They gracefully bear suffering.

   No criticism.

   Instruction: Be faithful until death.

   Promise: They would receive the crown of life.

3. PERGAMOS (Revelation 2:12-17)

   Commendation: They keep the faith of Christ.

   Criticism: They tolerate immorality, idolatry, and heresies.

   Instruction: Repent.

   Promise: Hidden manna and a stone with a new name.

4. THYATIRA (Revelation 2:18-29)

   Commendation: Their love, service, faith, patience is greater than at first.

   Criticism: They tolerated cult of idolatry and immorality.

   Instruction: Judgment was coming; keep the faith.

   Promise: They would to rule over nations and receive morning star.

5.   SARDIS (Revelation 3:1-6)

Commendation: Some have kept the faith.

Criticism: They had become a dead church.

Instruction: Repent and strengthen what remains.

Promise: The faithful would be honored and clothed in white.

6.   PHILADELPHIA (Revelation 3:7-13)

Commendation: Continued perseverance in faith.

Absolutely no criticism.

Instruction: Keep the faith.

Promise: A place in God's presence, a new name, and the New Jerusalem.

7.   LAODICEA (Revelation 3:14-22)

No commendation.

Criticism was indifferent.

Instruction: Become zealous and repent.

Promise: To share Christ's throne.

(REF. SFLB)

Which church do you think is your modern-day church? Why?

____

____

____

____

____

____

What should you do to make changes for the best?

____

____

____

____

____

____

NAME the seven churches here and repeat out loud as you write.

1. _______________________________________

2. _______________________________________

3. _______________________________________

4. _______________________________________

5. _______________________________________

6. _______________________________________

7. _______________________________________

The significance of the seven churches in Revelation is that each church is promised that everyone who conquers will be rewarded by Christ. Some historicists typically interpret the seven churches as representing seven different periods in the history of the western church from the time of Paul until the return of Jesus Christ. The church today is to promote fellowship, trust, faith, and hope, especially at this horrific time in world history. The pandemic, the Russian/Ukraine war, many types of various bugs springing forth from the coronavirus, and talks of nuclear war and recession… This most certainly is a time for Christians everywhere to PRAY earnestly.

June 12, 2022: Russia is still pounding Ukraine with artillery. PRAY.

The Twelve Tribes of Israel

The Israelites were the 12 sons of the biblical patriarch Jacob. Jacob had a daughter, Dinah, whose descendants were not recognized as a separate tribe. The sons of Jacob were born in Padan-Aram from different mothers, as follows:

1.   The sons of Leah: Reuben (Jacob's first born), Simeon, Levi, Judah, Issachar, and Zebulun.
2.   The sons of Rachel: Joseph and Benjamin (Jacob's last born).
3.   The sons of Bilhah, Rachel's handmaid: Dan and Naphtali.
4.   The sons of Zilpah, Leah's handmaid: Gad and Asher.

Reuben	Simeon	Levi
Judah	Issachar	Zebulun
Joseph	Benjamin	Dan
Naphtali	Gad	Asher

REPEAT out loud to yourself several times, then WRITE each one and name his mother:

1.______________________   Mother: ____________________

2.   ____________________   Mother: ____________________

3.   ____________________   Mother: ____________________

4. ________________ Mother: ________________

5. ________________ Mother: ________________

6. ________________ Mother: ________________

7.________________ Mother: ________________

8. ________________ Mother: ________________

9. ________________ Mother: ________________

10. ________________ Mother: ________________

11. ________________ Mother: ________________

12. ________________ Mother: ________________

Reuben	Simeon	Levi
Judah	Issachar	Zebulun
Joseph	Benjamin	Dan
Naphtali	Gad	Asher

ONCE AGAIN, REPEAT AND WRITE:

1. ________________ 7. ________________

2. ________________ 8. ________________

3. ________________ 9. ________________

4. ________________ 10. ________________

5. ________________ 11. ________________

6. ________________ 12. ________________

WHY ARE THE 12 TRIBES IMPORTANT TO US TODAY?

Knowledge of the 12 tribes of Israel is important because it helps us to understand current day situations. We have a greater insight as to WHY there is always UNREST in the Middle East. We see why it is always in the United States' best interest to be a friend to Israel because God has always promised to protect them. God will bless those who bless Israel and curse those who curse Israel (Genesis 12:3). This promise is for Christians also. God will bless those who bless us, and God will curse those who curse us. We understand better why the people of Israel have enemies because it was this way in the beginning. It is safe to assume that turmoil in the Middle East will continue until the return of Jesus Christ. It also helps us to understand why there may be a gathering of Israel.

To reinforce your faith, this is a paragraph from the Jewish Historian, Josephus. He lived during the life of Christ and wrote concerning what he saw, heard, and observed.

> *About this time there lived Jesus, a wise man, if indeed one ought to call him a man. For he was one who wrought surprising feats and was a teacher of such people as accept the truth gladly. He won over many Jews and many of the Greeks. He was the Messiah. When Pilate, upon hearing him accused by men of the highest standing among us, had condemned him to be crucified, those who had in the first place come to love (him) did not cease. On the third day he appeared to them restored to life. For the prophets of God had prophesied these and myriads of other marvelous (things) about him. And the tribe of the Christians, so called after him, has still up to now, not disappeared.*

This testimony acquired cardinal importance for the Christian church since it was first quoted by Eusebius of Caesarea (260-339) in his *History of the Church*. Its importance lies in the fact that it was considered reliable evidence for Jesus' divine nature, passion, and messiahship. Such testimony coming from a Jewish historian, who wrote shortly after Jesus' time, was thought to be convincing evidence for the discussions held between Jews and Christians in the early centuries of Christianity. No wonder, therefore, that it was reproduced time and again and used intensively by Christian authors as decisive and solid proof for Jesus' messiahship.

(REF. Josephus, Judaism and Christianity book, Chapter 16, p. 338)

The Five I Am's of Jesus

1. I AM the bread of life (John 6:48).

2. I AM the good shepherd (John 10:14).

3. I AM the light of the world (John 8:12).

4. I AM the resurrection and the life (John 11:25).

5. I AM the way, the truth and the life (John 14:6).

Mankind Has a Clear View

For since the creation of the world

His invisible attributes are clearly seen,

being understood by the things that are made,

even His eternal power and Godhead,

so that they are without excuse.

– Romans 1:20

NOTE: In looking at the created world, every person should see abundant evidence of God's existence and power.

Do Not Be a Fool

Psalm 14:1:

The Bible declares that the fool has said in his heart, "There is no God." REREAD the above paragraphs; they give total evidence of the reality of God's Son, Jesus, who came to Earth and completed the work that the Father had given Him to accomplish; DEATH on the cross to pay the penalty for the sin of mankind. PRAISE GOD, He paid your debt and my debt. What a glorious celebration we can have.

FIVE traits of a worldly walk are summed up in the word FUTIL-ITY (emptiness, purposelessness):

1. Darkened understanding;
2. Alienation from God;
3. Ignorance of God's ways;
4. A hardened heart; and
5. An unfeeling state.

YOU ARE NOW a new creation in Christ. But you have not so learned Christ, if indeed you have heard Him and have been taught by Him, as the truth is in Jesus that you put off concerning your former conduct; the old man who grows corrupt according to the deceitful lusts; and be renewed in the spirit of your mind, and that you put on the new man, who was created according to God, in true righteousness and holiness. (Ephesians 4:20-24, SFLB).

There is therefore now no condemnation
to those who are in Christ Jesus,
who do not walk according to the flesh,
but according to the Spirit.

For the LAW OF THE SPIRIT of life in Christ Jesus
has made me free from the law of sin and death.
– Romans 8:1-2, SFLB.

NOTE: Christians are free from God's banishing judgment. The law here is talking about the system of operation that the Spirit of life, the Holy Spirit, carries out in our lives, breaking the dominion of the old law, which is sin and death.

THIS IS IMPORTANT FOR ALL NEW BELIEVERS:

Do you not know that the unrighteous
will not inherit the kingdom of God?

DO NOT BE DECEIVED, neither fornicators,
nor idolaters, nor adulterers, nor homosexuals,
nor sodomites, nor thieves, nor covetous, nor drunkards,
nor revilers, nor extortioners will inherit the kingdom of God.
AND SUCH WERE SOME OF YOU.
But you were WASHED, but you were SANCTIFIED,
but you were JUSTIFIED in the name of the Lord Jesus
and by the Spirit of our God.
– 1 Corinthians 6:9-11

NOTE: Evildoers such as those mentioned by Paul can be fully cleansed from sin, WASHED, set apart for God, SANCTIFIED, and totally accepted in His holy sight, JUSTIFIED because some of the Corinthian Christians had known such lifestyles in their past. But their conversion was in the name of the Lord Jesus and by the Spirit of our God. The saving work of Christ is the ground on which the Holy Spirit is the agent through whom salvation is accomplished. He ends on a positive note, calling them to live according to who they are. (REF. SFLB)

NOTE: The apostle Paul was a murderer of Christians before his conversion to Christianity. Be assured, God loves you and desires that you make heaven your eternal home. Jesus will accept you out of any lifestyle and make you His very own.

IMPORTANT NOTE: Regarding 1 Corinthians 6:9-11:

- WASHED means cleansed from sin.
- SANCTIFIED means set apart for God.
- JUSTIFIED means totally accepted in His holy sight.

He who calls you is faithful, who also will do it.
- 1 Thessalonians 5:24

NOTE: God's faithfulness gives assurance that they (believers) will BE PRESERVED BLAMELESS until the return of Christ (v. 23). That means you. Making a choice to follow Jesus is the most important and exciting decision you will make in your entire lifetime. FAITH is simpler than it seems. It is a choice rather than an ability.

Ten Inspirational Characters from the Bible

TEN INSPIRATIONAL CHARACTERS FROM THE BIBLE

These men will inspire your personal faith.

MOSES, the man of patience. Moses had an encounter with God in the burning bush, which led him to help the Israelites escape from slavery in Egypt. He led them to Mount Sinai and received the Ten Commandments on stone tablets, which established the basic for Jewish Law. He was 120 years old when he died. He led the Israelites 40 years in the desert.

ABRAHAM. He was the first Hebrew patriarch and is revered in Judaism, Christianity, and Islam. He was called by God to travel to a new land, where he founded a nation. He was the first person to teach the idea that there is only ONE GOD.

NOAH was faithful, idealistic, strong, good looking, a poet, and helpful to those in need. He had a strong relationship with family and friends. In the story of the deluge, Genesis 6:11-9:19, he is represented as the patriarch who, because of his blameless piety, was chosen by God to perpetuate the human race after his wicked contemporaries had perished in the flood. After the flood, he became a farmer. He had three sons: Shem, Ham, and Japheth. His name means REST, and he had unwavering FAITH.

ELIJAH. A Hebrew prophet who ranks with Moses in saving the religion of Yahweh from being corrupted by the nature worship of Baal. He is an example of godliness and might. He also had struggles and doubts but remained faithful. We can receive assurance about who God is and what we can expect from him. Elijah was truthful, had courage, kindness, faithfulness and trust, and was responsible, loyal, and obedient. He was also one of two prophets who appeared with JESUS on the Mount of Transfiguration.

DANIEL was a man of devotion. He was a faithful servant of Yahweh living in Babylonian exile. The message of Daniel is that the God of Israel saved Daniel and his friends from their enemies, so he would save all Israel in their present oppression. This book makes it clear that the One True God is the Supreme Ruler over heaven and Earth. (Daniel 4:17)

DAVID was a strong and unassuming shepherd who became God's choice to replace Saul as King of Israel. David was humble yet self-possessed, readily dismissing human opinion. David trusted not his armors nor his soldiers; his dependence was entirely on God: God was his rock and fortress, the Lord was his Shepherd, the Lord was his light and salvation, the Lord was his strength and shield, the Lord was his trust. David was not a man after God's own heart because of his qualifications but because of the Lord's. He was a human being, like as are today, who came to realize that he needed a savior. He repented before God, just as we have to repent and accept God's forgiveness of sin by Jesus Christ.

JOB, a man of perseverance. He was a prosperous man of outstanding piety. Satan acted as an agent provocateur to test whether or not Job's piety is rooted in his prosperity. But Job, faced with the appalling loss of his possessions, his children, and his own health, remained faithful to God. Job is praised for his perseverance in the Christian Epistle of James. He is the protagonist of the pseudepigraphal book called the Testament of Job. Job suffered while innocent. Job questioned God.

> Job. 7:20: Job's loved ones did not help.
> Job 2:9: Job was restored.
> Job 42:10: Job kept his faith.

A lesson we can learn from Job is that no matter life's circumstances, maintaining FAITH is a possibility. Whether we are spiritually, emotionally, or physically stricken, we can keep our trust in God. He will at some point deliver us from trouble and make us better from the experience.

NOTE: "PROTAGONIST" is a leading character in a literary work. "PSEUDEPIGRAPHAL" refers to works purported to be written by noted authorities in either the Old/New Testaments or by persons involved in Jewish or Christian religious study or history.

SHADRACH, MESHACH, ABEDNEGO were underdogs. Now, these three figures from the biblical book of Daniel, Chapter 3, were thrown into a fiery furnace by Nebuchadnezzer II, King of Babylon, for refusing to bow down to the king's image. The moral of this story is that these men were totally committed to their faith, even when faced with a painful death. Because of their faith, GOD delivered them from evil. This deliverance from God for the three men brought the mighty king to recognize God's Lordship over Heaven and Earth.

NOTE: A person's character should not be based on their past but on how they get up and move forward.

New Jerusalem, Your Eternal Home

IF you have repented of your sin and received Jesus as Lord, you are on your way to the New Jerusalem.

1. It is called "New Jerusalem" (Revelation 21:2).
2. It is HOLY (Revelation 21:3).
3. It comes "down out of heaven."
4. It is prepared (Revelation 21:2).
5. It is God's dwelling place among men (Revelation 21:3).
6. There will be no death, mourning, or pain (Revelation 22:3).
7. It is for the VICTORIOUS (Revelation 21:7).
8. It is the Bride of Christ (Revelation 21:2; 9-10).
9. It shines with the Glory of God (Revelation 21:11-23).
10. It is the Ultimate Temple.

NOTE: It is a perfect cube of pure gold. It has 12 gates, each made of one giant pearl; it has 12 angels at the gates. The gates feature the names of the 12 tribes of Israel. It has 12 foundations of:

1. Jasper	2. Sapphire
3. Chalcedony	4. Emerald
5. Sardonyx	6. Sardius
7. Chrysolite	8. Beryl

9. Topaz   10. Chrysoprase

11. Jacinth   12. Amethyst

(Revelation 21:19-20)

The foundations feature the names of the 12 apostles you learned in a previous lesson. The city is 12,000 stadia long, wide, and high. Its walls are 144 cubits thick and made of jasper (Revelation 21). YOU do not want to miss this eternal destination/home.

GOD has chosen you, new believer, as His very own. Scripture says, you did not choose Him, but He chose you and appointed you that you should go and bear fruit, and that your fruit should remain; that whatever you ask the Father in Jesus's name, He will give it to you (John 15:16). SO ASK BIG. God is a big God, and He desires that you dream big.

Believers are:
1. Chosen – One who is the object of choice or Divine favor. You are exclusive, fancied, and one of choice.
2. Royal – Used to indicate that something is connected with a king, queen, or emperor, or their families. We, or believers, are in a royal family because we believe in Jesus.
3. A Holy Nation – God in His righteousness undid all the dysfunctional family slaves. He turned them into a Holy Nation, a private Kingdom. Holy Nation means they were a fully functional society not just spiritually. "Holy Nation" is a title which all win who wait worthily in the Lord's vineyard in their last days.

This is my way of personally fulfilling the great commission: "GO YE" into all the world and tell. Let people know of the mercy, grace, love, and forgiveness of our Lord Jesus Christ. No matter the deepest, dark, sick, immoral sin you have found yourself, God will forgive, cleanse, and make you completely whole.

Repent, believe, and receive. My dream/prayer is that God will allow me to see my little book go worldwide before He takes me home to Glory. It is my desire to let humanity know what JESUS did in my personal life.

The names on the twelve gates in the New Jerusalem are:
On the North, Reuben, Judah and Levi.
On the East, Joseph, Benjamin and Dan.
On the South, Simeon, Issachar and Zebulun.
On the West, Gad, Asher and Naphtali.
(Eze. 48:31-34)
The name of this city is, THE LORD IS THERE.

We will work in Heaven; but, the Bible is not clear
as to what type of work will be needed.

"Always give yourself fully to the work of the Lord,
because you know that your labor in the Lord is not in vain.
1 Cor. 15:58

Epilogue

It has been my pleasure to put together this book, *WHERE DO THEY FIT?*, of teaching, concerning God's word. My prayer is that you will go over and over the information in this booklet until it has sunk very deep within your heart. The Christian walk is not easy, but it is worth it. Keep your eyes on Jesus; CERTAINLY NOT MAN!

My little book can fit in your purse very easily. Keep it handy to read at home, at beauty shop, doctor's office—anywhere. *WHERE DO THEY FIT?* can be with you, right at your fingertips, 24/7. Remember, God loves you much more than you love yourself. Thank you for buying my book.

May God bless you exceedingly, abundantly, and above anything you could think or ask for having the desire to learn about God's book: the Bible.

See you in heaven!

The most famous Christian hymn is:
Amazing Grace by John Newton, a slave trader.
England 1779

Final Thoughts: The Story of Jonah

One of my very favorite Bible stories is Jonah. Now this man was so much like human beings today. He was rebellious against God and did not want to do His work. YET God called him a prophet...WHAT? This rebellious, non-compassionate, indifferent human being with a sour attitude on life was a prophet of God? The scripture says that is what God called him—a prophet. Well, God called Jonah to go to Nineveh and preach repentance to the people of this large city. Nineveh was a symbol of all future nations who refused to acknowledge the God of Israel as the only true God and turned to false gods that corrupted its life from within. Today, Nineveh is known as Iraq and Iran.

Was Jonah thrilled that God wanted to use him? No, not at all. HE ran the opposite direction and boarded a ship for another city named Tarshish, hoping God could not find him. Well, aboard the ship, God caused a horrific storm to come up and almost destroyed the ship. The men aboard the ship wondered why this storm had come upon them. They cast lots, and the lot fell on Jonah... So, he had to confess and let them know he was running from God. So they tossed much cargo overboard, trying to calm the storm, but nothing.

Jonah said: "Throw me overboard," and they finally did toss him over the side of the ship. To their amazement, the storm became calm.

God had prepared a big fish to swallow up Jonah. He spent three nights in the deep inside the belly of this great fish. How did he breathe? How did he survive? Scripture does not explain.

After three nights in the fish, Jonah called out to God, and God heard him and had the great fish spit him out on the shore. Still Jonah was reluctant because he knew God and knew that if the people repented, God would spare them. Even being reluctant, Jonah went into Nineveh and preached repentance. Sure enough, the people repented; they fasted and prayed, all the people and their cattle. God relented on wiping them out, and because of their repentance, God spared the whole city of about 120,000 people.

Was Jonah happy that God had spared the city? NO, not at all. He was angry and upset that God had shown mercy and forgiveness. Even after his three nights in the belly of the fish, Jonah still had a nasty/rebellious attitude. He wanted God to wipe those rebellious people off the face of the Earth. As we all do, seeing the gnat in someone's else eye but, not seeing the plank in our own. It was easy for Jonah to see the rebellion in Nineveh's people but not his own rebellion.

Well, Jonah decided to go eastward of the city to find a place to camp and have a pity party. Yes, the prophet of God had an ugly pity party. In his heart, he still wanted God to destroy Nineveh. God caused a plant to grow in order to shade Jonah, and then overnight, he caused a worm to eat it. Jonah awoke and was complaining about his living conditions, so God said to him: "You are all concerned and upset because I caused a wind/worm to destroy your habitat. Should I not be much more concerned about the well being of 120,000 residents of Nineveh?"

Now this man, Jonah, was one unique character. He was still rebellious/non-caring after God's judgement had fallen on him.

The moral of this story is that God has no problem removing you from your comfort zone. You can't run from God. Disobedience will cause turmoil in your life. With repentance comes obedience. We must learn to see the big picture and have a soft heart. YES, this story was an illustration of how many days Jesus would be in the tomb, but still it is the unique/unusual/mysterious story of a rebellious man who did not know that God was everywhere all the time.

NOTE: God used this man, Jonah, in a great and mighty way. It is our assurance that God can and will use us to pour forth His glory upon humanity. God knows your name, just like He knew Jonah. God has a good plan and purpose for your personal life.

You will learn to love the scriptures; they tell us some very interesting stories.

DO NOT disagree with God when He impresses upon your heart to work in/for His kingdom. He will give you the idea, the strength, the patience, the means, and the courage to go forward with great anticipation.

Lesson Answer Key

LESSON 1

1. Moses

2. 1,500

3. 40

4. 66

5. The coming of Jesus

6. The life and works of Jesus

7. True

8. True

LESSON 2

LESSON 1 REVIEW QUESTIONS

1. 40

2. 5

3. 66

4. 39

5. 1,500

6. Genesis, Exodus, Leviticus, Numbers, Deuteronomy, Joshua, Judges, Ruth, 1 Samuel and 2 Samuel.

LESSON 2 NEW MATERIAL

1. 3

2. Hebrew, Aramaic, Greek

3. Gutenberg

4. Psalms

5. Ezra

6. Job

7. 66

8. 39

LESSON 3

LESSONS 1-2 REVIEW

1. Moses

2. 66

3. 39

4. Gutenberg

5. True; Hebrew, Aramaic, Greek

LESSON 3 NEW MATERIAL

Books that do not belong in the Old Covenant:

Revelation; Luke; Acts; 1 John; Mark; John; Romans; Jude

LESSON 4

1. 40

2. 1,500

3. Moses

4. 5

5. Genesis, Exodus, Leviticus, Numbers, Deuteronomy

6. 39

7. Malachi

LESSON 5

Books that do not belong in the New Covenant:
Amos; Jonah; Numbers; Ester; Genesis; Ruth

LESSON 6

Brief Test (O.T. or N.T.?)

Hebrews – N.T.	Genesis – O.T.
Numbers – O.T.	Titus – N.T.
James – N.T.	Job – O.T.
Proverbs – O.T.	Ezra – O.T.
Esther – O.T.	Luke – N.T.
Acts – N.T.	Hosea – O.T.
Philemon – N.T.	Romans – N.T.
Ezekiel – O.T.	Song of Solomon – O.T.